Song of the North

Poem by FRANK ASCH   *Photographs by* TED LEVIN

A GULLIVER GREEN BOOK HARCOURT BRACE & COMPANY

San Diego   New York   London

Printed in Singapore

Salmon knows how to spawn in northern lakes.
Salmon knows how to swim to the sea.
Salmon knows many things. . . .

But who knows Salmon
and the song she sings?

Walrus knows how to feast on clams from the ocean floor.
Walrus knows how to bask in the northern sun.
Walrus knows many things. . . .

But who knows Walrus
and the song she sings?

Puffin knows how to nest on northern cliffs.
Puffin knows how to dive and swim.
Puffin knows many things. . . .

But who knows Puffin
and the song she sings?

Dall sheep knows how to graze on northern slopes.
Dall sheep knows how to listen for Wolf.
Dall sheep knows many things. . . .

But who knows Dall sheep
and the song she sings?

Caribou knows how to forage alone.
Caribou knows when to follow the northern sun.
Caribou knows many things. . . .

But who knows Caribou
and the song she sings?

Moose knows the taste of northern ponds.
Moose knows how to protect her young.
Moose knows many things. . . .

But who knows Moose
and the song she sings?

Bear knows how to catch Salmon.
Bear knows how to sleep through northern winters.
Bear knows many things. . . .

But who knows Bear
and the song she sings?

The Land of the North knows many songs:
Salmon, Walrus, Puffin, Dall sheep,
Caribou, Moose, and Bear . . .

But who listens to the Land of the North?
Who hears the song she sings?

For Alison
—F. A.

For Jordan, who loved the "bou"
—T. L.

The animals included in this book are listed below
in order of appearance from left to right:

Atlantic puffin

Pink salmon
Pink salmon
Sockeye salmon
Pink salmon and glaucous-winged gulls
Humpback whale

Walrus
Walrus
Walrus
Walruses
Polar bears (mother and cub)

Horned puffin
Atlantic puffin
Tufted puffin
Horned puffins
Immature bald eagle

Dall sheep (ewe)
Wolf
Dall sheep (ram)
Dall sheep (lambs)
Hoary marmot

Barren ground caribou (bull)
Barren ground caribou (bull)
Barren ground caribou (cows)
Barren ground caribou (bull)
Short-eared owl

Moose cow and calves
Moose (cow)
Moose cow and calves
Bull moose
Beaver

Kodiak brown bear
Kodiak brown bear
Grizzly bears
Grizzly bear
Red fox pup (black phase)

Library of Congress Cataloging-in-Publication Data
Asch, Frank.
Song of the north/written by Frank Asch; photographs by Ted Levin.
p. cm.
"Gulliver Green Books."
ISBN 0-15-201258-3
1. Zoology—Arctic regions—Juvenile poetry. 2. Children's poetry, American.
3. Animals—Juvenile poetry.
I. Levin, Ted. II. Title.
PS3551.S3S6 1999
811'.54—dc21   97-50161

First edition
F E D C B A

Gulliver Green® books focus on various aspects of ecology and the environment,
and a portion of the proceeds from the sale of these books is donated to protect, preserve,
and restore native forests.

The photographs in this book were taken in Alaska at Prince William Sound, Paxton Lake,
Round Island, Denali National Park, Kodiak Island, and Fairbanks; in Canada at Machias Seal
Island, New Brunswick and Hudson Bay, Manitoba; and off the coast of New Hampshire with
Nikon camera bodies and lenses, ranging from 24mm to 800mm, using a Gitzo tripod.
The film used was Fuji 50 and 100, Fuji Velvia, and Kodachrome 25-64.
The display type was set in Birch.
The text type was set in Goudy Sans Medium.
Color separations by United Graphic Pte. Ltd., Singapore
Printed and bound by Tien Wah Press, Singapore
This book was printed on totally chlorine-free Nymolla Matte Art paper.
Production supervision by Stanley Redfern
Designed by Kaelin Chappell